T0196438

OTHER BOOKS BY LUCKNER PIERRE:

Born Unloved

Nurture the Spirit of Your Humor

CPA Wisdom for Accounting & Business Students

POETRY LOVES BABIES, CHILDREN & TEENS

POETRY SERVES THE YOUTH

Luckner Pierre

authorHOUSE®

AuthorHouse™
1663 Liberty Drive
Bloomington, IN 47403
www.authorhouse.com
Phone: 1-800-839-8640

Published by AuthorHouse 3/22/2012

ISBN: 978-1-4685-5804-3 (sc)

This book is a work of non-fiction. Names of people and places have been changed to protect their privacy.

This book is printed on acid-free paper.

Dedicated to all the babies, children and teens. Also, dedicated to Kaden Eric Aumoitte. There's hope at school and at the playground. God's love is a divine inspiration.

Patience is the root of love. Only God's love can change the human heart.

Mission Statement: to share similar interests, realistic ideals, educational goals and positive experiences with "different people" and respect every culture

Vision Statement: to promote education, self-control and fellowship of love to humanity

"One who does not know his history is like a tree without roots."

-An African Quote

Confidence + Right Motivation = Preparation for Success

"The purest form of thinking in art is to believe the sense of everything as nothing and the sense of nothing as everything.

To playfully engage on both terms is to live a mind of a true child, the artist."

-Arthur Narvaez

5 senses:
sight
listen
smell
touch
taste

3 Pillars of Poetry:
1. emotion
2. image
3. music

The song is ended, but the melody lingers on.

-Author Unknown

"As a songwriter, I am often approached by people who say, "Your songs put into words exactly what's in my heart!' What a great privilege and responsibility it is to write lyrics that help people express what they are feeling.

Words are powerful.

I hope these cards help many of you express your heart to the ones you care about during important moments in your lives."

-Chris Rice

7 LEADERSHIP SKILLS:

1. Be Humble and Obedient

2. Be a Good Listener

3. Be a Servant

4. Encourage People to be Confident and Courageous

5. Develop a Zeal for Righteousness

6. Accept Challenges and Gain Spiritual Growth

7. Be an Open-Minded Leader

"Do not go where the path may lead go instead where there is no path and leave a trail."

-Ralph Waldo Emerson

H-Humor

A-Appreciation

P-Positive

P-Protagonist

Y-Yummy

L-Leadership

O-Optimistic

V-Vision

E-Encouragement

CONTENTS

SECTION 3 POEMS FOR TEENS

SECTION 4 MORE POEMS

ACKNOWLEDGEMENT

I gratefully thank Almighty Sovereign God for protecting me with His love, righteousness, grace and mercy.

Secondly, I generously want to thank Professor Albo (Queen of Modern Poetry). I want to thank Arthur Narvaez for his leadership in studying poetry and for his temperance. I want to thank my sister, all of my aunts and brother for their support. I want to thank Sensi Armando (Instructor) for his generosity to my teenage life. I thank Candence for her interest in poetry.

I thank all the parents, babies, children, teenagers, families, dishwashers, restaurant employees, volunteers, internees, business managers, sales clerks, social workers, cartographers, lifeguards, physicians, medical doctors, dentists, school patrol guards, school teachers, chaperons, positive role models, security guards, construction workers, water boys and water girls, cheerleaders including all professional cheerleaders, local playground employees, all the mascots, school teachers, video game companies, cereal companies, singers, rappers, music producers, studio engineers, librarians, library clerks, public speakers, vocational teachers, foreign language teachers and professors, educators, college tutors, college mentors, writers including poets, Academy of American Poets, accountants, every toy store including Toys "R" Us, Boys & Girls Club, every Job Corps vocational schools, Habitat for Humanity and every book publishing company including AuthorHouse that have contributed a labor of love to humanity.

I want to thank Aquil, Johnathan Pierre and Fernando Brown. I also want to thank those who believed in me and contributed to my spiritual growth and college career. I appreciate those who love me the right way. Thank you so much for your love and support. Life is what you make it. I love every nationality, country and ethnic background that exists in the earth. Every country has something beautiful to offer. Unconditional love overcomes jealousy, envy and hatred. It promotes true happiness. Embrace the arms of love. Everyone needs unconditional love. Let unconditional love help you maintain your integrity. Feel alive again by the breath of love. Love is unconditional.

INTRODUCTION

Since 2005, I have wanted to write a poetry book for children and teens. Seven years later, I finally published it at the right time. As a servant of poetry, I write poems to help people of all ages relate to humanity and to communicate an important message to the heart of people.

Although there is a low demand for poetry, poetry still exists in every country around the world. It's even found in GED testing.

Until today, the art of poetry communicates to the heart, mind and soul of children and teenagers. Even reading poetry to babies can help keep their neurons active and refresh to increase their IQ for the rest of their lives.

Equally important, every elementary, middle school and high school should offer a poetry class to teach the fundamentals of poetry. It would help increase their reading comprehension, IQ and help the youth enjoy life to the fullest. It would also give them a sense of true humility and prepare them to be servant boys and servant girls in the community and sharpen their creativity and give them a proactive approach to be productive and be sensitive to other peoples' feelings.

Every child and teenager comes from a different walk of life and everyone's social background and culture are different.

So what do all children have in common? They all live in the same planet that is surrounded by the clouds, skies and the sun shining on the earth several areas at a time. Some bar restaurants have open-mic events for poets and singers.

Whether it's traditional or modern poetry, poetry exercises

the human brain, releases emotional stress and nurtures the human soul. My college poetry professor once said, "A poet is a professor of all senses."

Early in the morning, I sometimes would write, read, breathe and eat poetry. It's a lifestyle. Limerick, a five-line poem, is usually the longest stanza in poems. The word "stanza" means room in Italian. Different languages of poetry taste like chocolate marshmallows. It's never too late to study and learn the art of poetry and how important it is to the human life.

I want people to feel connected and reconnected to the spirit of poetry at no cost. Read a poem to a child or teen before bedtime. Poetry will always be an academic skill in the heart of education and a rainbow of love. Let poetry serve the youth with unconditional love.

Now ask yourself, "Do people love me for who I am or do they love me based on a condition?

-Luckner Pierre

POEMS

FOR BABIES

Born Unloved

never felt love
by someone
who knows how to
love unconditionally

turn pain into power
anguish still blocks
like a hard rock
born unloved

Baby Muscles

gently hold a baby's hand
strong enough to
hold an adult
milk does a body good
strong baby muscles

ACTIVATE NEURONS

when a baby is born
activate the neurons
from the storm

play classical music
and sounds of nature
let it nuture the neurons

without neurons
pain begins to grow
like a volcano

BABY HUMOR

babies smile
like a rainbow
over the playground

sleep with a smile
wake up with a smile
of unconditional love

Happy Feet

happy feet
happy feet
feel happy
from the mind
to the feet

Chocolate Feeds My Dreams
dedicated to Kaden Eric Mouitte

chocolate brownies
chocolate cake
chocolate pizza
chocolate feeds my dreams

Babies Cry for Love

after birth
babies cry for love
and need comfort
at night

life begins with instructions
broken and damaged
rebuilt by love
life goes on

every baby
needs real love
only love gives meaning
to every baby life

Learn by Foot

walk by foot
let the brain
breathe and believe
positive energy will flow

every foot needs
arch support, pedicure and
love
learn by foot

Words to My Unknown Father
dedicated to all orphans

where am I?
inside of my mother's womb
born unloved
like a bird without feathers

where were you
when I was born?
alone in my struggle
put yourself in my shoe

what went wrong between
you and my mother?
different fathers with the same mother
my sister and brother

I never met you
or saw you
I had to learn
God is my only father

POEMS
FOR CHILDREN

LET'S BUILD A PLAYGROUND
dedicated to every city

imagine living
in a neighborhood
without a playground

where would the kids
have fun?
they need a fun playground

bring carpenters and painters
to help build a playground
let's build a playground

Nurture a Child's Talent

every child is born
with a gift of talent
be prepared for every challenge
maintain a healthy balance

intrinsic ability alone
lacks diligence and discipline
children need training
build on their endowment

be patient with their childhood
always remember
never be overprotective
nurture a child's talent

encouragement is
part of the fabric
of life
all day and night

humanity needs talented children
nurture the spirit of
a child's talent
a God's gift to humanity

CHILDREN ARE MEEK AND IDEALISTIC

never lay a hand
on children
when they make mistakes
encourage them

parents who embitter
their children
need to imitate
children's childlike humility

be meek and idealistic
receptive and optimistic
care for their needs
let them please God

no child is a slave
children need Kingdom Kids
trained them to have
godly ways

even adopted children
need encouragement
inherit the power of meekness
learn their weakness

every community needs playgrounds
where children have fun
and enjoy diversity
in a safe environment

STOP BULLYING ME

stop bullying me
stop bullying me
teachers mistaken me
for a problem child

fear grew from
my heart to my anus
I struggled with fear
Impossible to smile

bitter pain
shaved the skin
of my brain
like a razor blade

fear made me wild
anger made me hostile
in trouble for a while
impossible to smile

love was nowhere
to be found
like a lost crown
forced to be antisocial

stop bullying me
stop bullying me
monkey see monkey do
stop, stop, stop

Filtered Water

drink filtered water
clean like fresh air
enough hydration

animals and plants
need filtered water
and sunlight

live with clean water
fresh filtered water
tastes like pure rain

Pursue True Happiness

when personal struggles bubble
protect happiness from trouble
double the happiness

right motivation of happiness
imagine the possibility of hope
envision life on the other side

educate happiness
let it be your friend
let it bear fruit

even bums on the streets
need happiness to stay alive
tastes like medicine for the soul

never lose the courage of happiness
sincerely appreciate joy of happiness
share happiness with love

breathe an air of happiness
pursue true happiness
then let it cry

PROFOUND BOOKS

profound books promote
positive energy
like the journey of
a dream

in bookstores
at the table
feel the energy
of the authors

at home
keep bookshelves for
profound books
like a college library

dollars and cents
can't buy common sense
think big
reflect on profound books

RECYCLE THE EARTH

with clean plastic gloves
collect all garbages
recylce the world
with pure love

recycle paper
recycle plastic bottles
recycle soda cans

recycle every toy
adapt to recycle
recycle the earth with love

My Computer Bedroom

my bedroom
is like a computer
access to internet
for educational resources

posters of encouragement
on the wall
bookshelf filled with
profound books

like a playground
full of fun activities
I enjoy
my computer bedroom

SPELLING BEE

learn twenty words
per week
spell them in your sleep
vocabulary words in a dream

write each word
on an index card
carry them with you
win the spelling bee

CALENDAR

twelve months in a year
fifty-two weeks
three hundred sixty-five days
average of thirty days

even though time
is manmade
learn the amount of days
in each month

A Child Star
dedicated to Gary Coleman

any child
can be a star
sons and daughters
must be mature by discipline

every child needs encouragement,
moral guidance and self-discipline
patience is the key
heart of a champion

Home Encouragement

when children bring
a good report card
encourage them with love

replace discouragement with
encouragement
feel alive again

every home needs
encouragement or else
no positive reinforcement

DISNEYWORLD AND DISNEYLAND

visit Disneyworld
and Disneyland
meet Mickey Mouse
visit the house

ride in the boat
watch the musical performance
dance with friends
and family

BUSCH GARDENS
theme park vacation

visit Busch Gardens
in Tampa
enjoy the food
and games

Birthday Cake

thank mom and dad
make a wish
and blow the candle light

let mom or dad
help you cut the cake
and say to yourself, "Happy Birthday!"

Chocolate Marshmallows

imagine chocolate marshmallows
at the supermarkets
delicious for all holidays

mix with
peanut butter pancakes
or cupcakes

Tickle by the Pickle

pickle for the hotdogs
pickle for football sandwiches
tickle my teeth
tickle my tongue
tickle by the pickle

More than One Trade

choose three trades
serve an industry
and market your resume
learn more than one trade

MASCOT

every city needs
a mascot
cheers and laughs
heart of a champion

every team
needs a mascot
to help promote
a winning attitude

GOSPEL IN THE GHETTO

words of the gospel
reaches to evrey ghetto
like construction heavy metal
where workers settle

life in the ghetto
must begin with the gospel
within the resurrection of Christ
to revolutionize every human soul

as long as the
gospel of Christ is promoted
there can be
"Gospel Comedy Nights"

Young without Moral Guidance

without moral values
even a class in ethics
lacks discernment

moral values maintain
good conduct
value love, integrity and wisdom

without moral guidance
youngsters become
instruments of wickedness

victimized by lack of guidance
destroyed by the complacency
of fools

surround yourself with
open-minded leaders and
a wise mentor of righteousness

appreciate moral values
with a positive attitude
even parents need moral values

AIKIDO FOR KIDS

kids need self-control
aikido protects them
from class bullies

PAPER AND PENCIL AWAITS

paper and pencil awaits
for my hand to write
left to right

my eraser is finished
my pen ran out of
ink before I think

Tic-Tac-Toe

let's play
tic-tac-toe
make your head
talk to your toes

let's play
toe-tac-tic
make your skin
soft and itch

tic-tac-toe
toe-tac-tic
tic-tac-toe
toe-tac-tac

tic-tac—toe
toe-tac-tic
tic-tac-toe
toe-tac-tic

DEPRESSION LIVES ALONE

without a father
sad days await
in my room
depression lives alone

where would I be
without love?
sometimes I wish
I was never born

CPR FOR KIDS
dedicated to Red Cross

listen to the instructor
arms must be straight
oxygen, breath and cardiac
enjoy the lessons

analyze the rhythm
for the AED training device
only the doctor removes
the defrilbator

NEVER ABANDON A CHILD

every child needs unconditional love
after school they need a hug
after homework they need a hug
before bedtime they need a hug

children need encouragement
never abandon a child
it takes a village
to raise a child

POEMS
FOR TEENS

TEENAGERS ARE PEOPLE TOO!

full of zest for life
an abundance of energy
and love to have fun
teenagers are people too!

A VISION FOR TEENS

every teen needs a vision
a vision of discernment
a vision of unity
a vision of courage
a vision of integrity

every teen needs a vision
a vision of peace
a vision of unity
a vision of love
a vision of humilty

ADAPT TO DIVERSITY

learn to listen, read
and write another language
every word
is a symbol

learn at least
three languages
every place needs diversity
diversity promotes love

TOMBOY
inspired by the movie

a tomboy can teach
boys leadership values,
moral values and intellectual values
and still be a woman

she plays basketball, volleyball,
football, baseball and soccer
she finds her identity
in unconditional love

with courage and confidence
she defends herself
every playground needs a tomboy
to teach the boys a lesson

SURROUNDED BY FAVORITISM

surrounded by favoritism
most people don't care
adopt moral values
gain personal growth

resist the temptation of favoritism
anyone could be your family
a man reaps what he sows
keep a healthy personality from insanity

love shows no favoritism
replace favoritism with personal growth
at the end of the day
favoritism leads to a false impression

GED

clearly understand
reading and mathematics
lead to reasonable conclusions

Algebra and Geometry
teaches the mind
to calculate numbers

reading and writing
are closely related
teaching the meaning of words

measure the GED
with wisdom and discernment
education is preparation itself

Little Haiti Playground
Little Haiti in Miami

one day
on second avenue
I saw a playground
in Little Haiti

children and teens
can play soccer or football
on the grass
at Little Haiti Playground

Hands full of Dirt
dedicated to Haiti

when disaster struck Haiti
the earth was hurt
turned water into dirt

when disaster struck Haiti
the earth was hurt
hands full of dirt

hands full of dirt
carpenters and painters can
rebuild Haiti with many hands

KITCHEN INSURANCE

let me wash
all the dirty dishes
in the sink
and let me think

I like to wash
dirty dishes
even after the party
no more dirty dishes

INSPIRATIONAL MOVIES

inspirational movies
educate the human heart
and stimulate the mind

connect the breath of faith
with rational thinking
enlighten and encourage others

biblical stories for kids
heartwarming stories for adults
feed the soul with wisdom

feed the eyes with holiness
let the ears hear laughter
let the heart feel joy

Lifeguard is a Lifestyle

lifeguard
is a lifestyle
protect humanity
from danger

CPR and breathing techniques
are important at all times
every swimmer
should care

life of a lifeguard
saves lives
always wear a lifejacket and
be prepared for who is drowning

Plates, Pots and Pans
dedicated to all dishwashers

my hands are train
to wash plates, pots,
pans, forks and
spoons

a man once said,
"your hand can always
be washed even if
it's full of dirt"

Slave to a Cigarette

whoever invented cigarette
is a slave to ashes
don't be a slave
to a cigarette

Say No to Drugs

say no to drugs
no to drugs
say yes to love
addiction is a disease

MOUSE INSIDE THE BANK

in the bank office
a small mouse slowly
walked inside the bank

it ran into a hole
blocked by a small box
we laughed and laughed
mouse inside the bank

THINGS LOGIC CAN'T EXPLAIN

off course
every case
needs logic
and rational thinking

can logic explain
every past event?
can logic predict
the future?

logic can't explain
certain things like
money can't buy life,
health and love

CAN'T BUY FORGIVENESS

money can't buy forgiveness
not even
red roses and a letter
can buy forgiveness

forgiveness is from
the inside out
not from money
and materialism

never try to buy
her forgiveness
let her forgive
within unconditional love

Connected to Arthur Rimbaud
dedicated to Arthur Rimbaud

his mother mistreated him
built emotional damages
in his life
he became a martyr

a season in hell
damaged his social life
never a chance
to see the college life

like other writers,
Rimbaud developed
an intellectual life
in literature

whether in the past,
present or future
his vision connects
with my vision

NEVER UNDERESTIMATE ELDERS
dedicated to all elders

a young man
underestimated an elderly man
trained in karate
with wisdom

after they competed
the young man
was hurt and felt pain
never underestimate elders

NEVER UNDERESTIMATE WOMEN

too many men
underestimate women
the average woman is smarter
than the average man

short or tall
with any skin color
women are more vigilant
with a sharper intuition

I believe one day
there will be…
a female president
never underestimate women

BEACH LIFE

breathe the fresh air
at the beach
large rocks under the
water of the sea

play with the sand
build a sand castle
play football on the sand
run and tackle

fresh clean air
healthy for the lungs
enjoy the
beach life

A QUIET FOREST

fresh air breathes
early in the morning
clouds and the sky
smell like fresh water

PLAY THE GUITAR

play the guitar
acoustic or electric
with any musical voice

I can't imagine
life without a guitar
like oxygen and blood

with piano or violin
bass guitar is the
best solo instrument

FINANCIALLY DISCIPLINE

save money
in a piggy bank
and be
financially wise

money can't buy love
yet
save it for
a college education

"BAYSIDE"
dedicated to Laurie Noepel

dressed in pink
like pink roses
we walked to Bayside
like trusted friends

when she danced,
she said, "Boogie boogie,"
I held her hand
she felt protected

her gentle spirit
comes natural like fresh water
her hair is my comfort
her life is part of mine

UNLIKE JORDAN
dedicated to Michael Jordan

Jordan is unstoppable
like Jerry Rice
on the field

his performance even
encourages fans of other teams
to love him

let the children say,
"like Mike, if I could
be like Mike"

never compare other players
to Mike
Jordan revolutionized the game

DANCE LIKE A MOTORCYCLE

dance like a motorcycle
do the motorcycle
do the motorcycle
do the motorcycle

dance like a motorcycle
do the motorcycle
do the motorcycle
do the motorcycle

dance like a motorcycle
do the motorcycle
do the motorcycle
do the motorcycle

dance like a motorcycle
do the motorcycle
do the motorcycle
do the motorcycle

dance like a motorcycle
do the motorcycle
do the motorcycle
do the motorcycle

CONNECTED TO ANOTHER WORLD

would there be vitamins
and minerals in another world?
or would there
just be contaminated water?

would there be sports
in another world
or would there be
deserted places?

would there be doctors and
nurses in another world?
or would there
just be a scientist?

would there be moral laws
and freedom in another world?
or would there be
chaos and destruction?

would there be music
in another world?
or would there be
unconditional love?

men are from Mars
women are from Venus
connect Mars and to Venus
connected to another world

ALL SCHOLARSHIPS LOVE EDUCATION

scholarships await
for students who are
serious for the college life

write essays
write book reports
write scholarly articles

adapt to diversity
all scholarships
love education

SALVATION EMBRACES BLACK HISTORY

what does Black History
mean to you?
transform the human nature
redemption leads to victory

enrich the spirit of history
educate and nurture it
bear good fruits
rebuild the educational system with love

where there are culture
salvation purifies and cures all flaws
a ministry of salvation in every nation
serves every culture out of love

salvation maintains integrity of history
strengthen by grace and overcome disgrace
black history needs spiritual nourishment
a multicultural side

Ms. President

imagine every country
have a female president
she would lead
like a pilot

people say,
"it's not possible."
anything is possible
it's a woman's world!

Honesty Builds Confidence

children need confidence to succeed
protect them from danger
when they meet a stranger

honesty helps them believe
in academic success
builds the trust of love

BE GRATEFUL

never lose the spirit of gratitude
embrace an attitude of gratitude
appreciate childhood and teenage years

at the end of every year
count all of your blessings
have fun
be grateful for what God has done

FEEL YOUNG AGAIN

rejuvenate the youth
feel young again
reality teaches everyone the truth

enjoy the spirit of youth
be happy and joyful
renew the heart of youth

feel young and unashamed
set an excellent example
actions speak louder than words

never lose the integrity of youth
rejuvenate the days of youth
everyone needs to feel young again

LIVE BY TRUTH

truth awaits
live by truth
love the truth
truth implies truth

in the morning
in the afternoon
at night
live by truth

MORE
P O E M S

A Mistake by the Lake

there was a mistake
by the lake
I walked on an
ice cold lake

birds are saying,
"I can walk
on water
at this lake"

again, I walked on an
ice cold lake
was it a mistake
or a fake lake?

The Popcorn Walk

walk like a popcorn
pop and pop
like a blow pop

pop, pop and pop
microwave or stove
walk like a popcorn

Candy Brain

candy brain tastes richly sweet
caramel with nuts and sugar
for short-term memory
and long-term memory
every brain needs candy brain

Fish Brain

eat fish
let it swim
in your brain

eat fish
let it strengthen the mind
and tease the brain

eat fish
fish swallows migraines,
headaches and emotional pain

after I ate some fish
I can't imagine life
without a fish brain

CONSCIOUS OF A POET
dedicated to every poet

is the conscious
of a poet awake?
when is the conscious
spiritually awake?

let intuition
sharpen conscious
let wisdom open the
eyes of conscious

train the conscious
of a poet
to meditate
like yoga

does the conscious
of a poet
understand every society
in the world?

CARPENTRY IS A LEADER
dedicated to Habitat for Humanity

carpentry is wise
and a leader to humanity
carpentry teaches children
how to build homes

roof over the head
floor for the bed
and home-resistant walls
for wicked weather

with active listening
carpentry is an
open-minded leader
who honors every carpenter

POETRY BORN AGAIN

poetry gave music
a natural voice
never ends
now born again

destiny of poetry
prospers every song
wait…
poetry is born again

EARS OF THE HEART

some people want to
hear what their ears
want to hear

ears of the heart
need to grasp instructions
like a divine interruption

harden hearts
cannot hear the truth
blocked by many sins

a new heart
feels refresh and rest
in the attitude of gratitude

your heart is
your own worst enemy
let God be the remedy

TROPHY OF HONOR

a trophy honors
confidence and courage
a trophy represents
reverence and leadership

when someone gives
a trophy of honor
always remember it as
a symbol of hope

IN TOUCH WITH LOVE

reality is in touch
with love
within every heartbeat
penetrate the soul

love understands
every situation
in the world
in and out

receptive to realistic ides
nurture the world
love is in touch
with reality

BREATH OF LOVE

take a deep breath
breathe, breathe
breath of love
lives in mankind

breathe, breathe
let love enter the
heart and lungs
new life instead of old

love breathes fresh air
around the earth
every place
needs love

breath of love
is like chicken soup
for the soul
God's breath is love

GOD'S RESUME

God's objective aims
to renew the heart
of every person

His education offers
theology, Christian law schools
and holiness

RESOURCES:

BOOKS:

Poetry Matters (Writing a Poem From the Inside Out) by Ralph Fletcher

Poem-Making: Ways to Begin Writing Poetry by Myra Cohn Livingston

A Season in Hell by Arthur Rimbaud (Translated by Louise Varese)

The Rose that Grew from Concrete by Tupac Shakur

Intimacies: Poems of Love by Pablo Neruda

Selected Writings by Jose Marti

WEBSITES:

www.poets.org

ABOUT THE AUTHOR:

Since his college days, Pierre has been an inspirational writer.

Pierre earned an AA degree in Accounting. He has adapted to different subject matters, such as poetry, sports, accounting and spiritual-related topics.

Pierre has written seven books in his writing career. His insightful thinking helped him realize he can write poetry and literary books about his real-life experiences with realistic concepts to encourage everyone in the world.

Pierre has a love and passion for writing books. His intelligence and integrity earned him the leadership role who can lead people to victory, academic success, encourage people to break free from cultural barriers and love the good side of people.

His books will continue to impress, inspire, and motivate others for generations to come.